My Little RESPECTFUL ROBOT

PETER PAUPER PRESS, INC.
Rye Brook, New York

PETER PAUPER PRESS

In 1928, at the age of twenty-two, Peter Beilenson began printing books on a small press in the basement of his parents' home in Larchmont, New York. Peter—and later, his wife, Edna—sought to create fine books that sold at "prices even a pauper could afford."

Today, still family owned and operated, Peter Pauper Press continues to honor our founders' legacy of quality, value, and fun for big kids and small kids alike.

Written by Hannah Beilenson
Designed by Heather Zschock

3 International Drive
Rye Brook, NY 10573 USA

Published in the UK and Europe by Peter Pauper Press, Inc.
c/o White Pebble International
Units 2-3, Spring Business Park
Stanbridge Road
Havant, Hampshire PO9 2GJ, UK

ISBN 978-1-4413-4209-6
Printed in China

7 6 5 4 3 2 1

OUR ACTIONS AND US

Have you ever tried something new? Shared a toy or snack? Given a hug or high five when someone needed it? Well, those are just a few examples of putting your feelings into action! And every action you take can make a change. You can make people smile and laugh, help others feel safe, and create something new for everyone to share. There's so much you can do, and there's no wrong place to start—so let's take action today!

One action is **Respect**, and we'll meet someone who will help us learn more about it.

It's my turn to play with the train set!

You played with it yesterday.
It's my turn to use it!

That doesn't sound very respectful!

I'm a **Respectful Robot**!
I teach you about respect.

Respect means treating others in a way that makes them feel cared for.

I'm not sure how to do that.

Well, how do people show you that they care?

Well, Dad always checks under the bed for monsters.

And I like when our teacher reads
us stories in the afternoon.

But I'm afraid of monsters.
And I'm not that good at reading.

AND I'M MAD
AT YOU!

Sometimes when you’re mad,
it can be hard to show respect.

But when you listen and
don't interrupt,

or when you use words and don't kick or hit,

you can show that you care even
when you're angry or annoyed.

I'm sorry, too!

Sharing is a great way of showing respect, and so is saying sorry when you've hurt someone's feelings.

Oh, I think I understand. Respect means treating people how you'd like to be treated.

Yeah! So when
I take turns,

and when I follow the rules,

and when I take
care of my things,

that's us showing respect!
Thanks for teaching us.
No problem—now let's get back to playing!

Meet My Respectful Robot

My Respectful Robot's name is:

....

I feel cared for when:

....

....

....

I can show respect by:

....

....

....

....